THE GUIDES TO THE PROPHETIC HOUSEHOLD

SAQIBI SEIF

ISBN: 978-1-990751-30-1

CONTENTS

DEDICATION

I dedicate this book to Sayyidina Mustafa Ahmed Muhammad ﷺ and the Ahl Al Bayt and Ale Muhammad, may we be continuously embraced by their lights, the essence of our good fate, Ameen x3 who/Hu هو are always for The Best. I also dedicate this book to all of their lovers and knowers aka the AwliyaAllah. But I ultimately dedicate this book to everyone who/Hu هو wishes to purify their inward realties, who/Hu هو desire to be close to the presence of Haqq حق, Divine Truth, The Best and so therefore may each reading of this book be a means of immense blessings for us all in the here and now, in the grave, and in the hereafter.

Ameen x3

ACKNOWLEDGEMENTS

First and foremost, I thank and acknowledge Allah ﷲ, The One Supreme, The Best, for allowing me to write such couplets in the honor and love of the Ahl Al Bayt and Ale Muhammad, may we be continuously embraced by their lights, the essence of our good fate, Ameen x3, the Awliyallah, for without Allah ﷲ, The One Supreme, The Best, supporting and allowing me to write such couplets this would not have come into existence. Secondly, I thank and acknowledge Sayyeda Alicia Ali who/Hu هو was generous enough to help publish my books. Thirdly, I thank my editor, Mehtab Alvi and everyone who/Hu هو has worked on this book, without them this book wouldn't have been possible.

May Allah ﷲ, The One Supreme, The Best, accept this humble labor of love for His love.

Ameen x3

PREFACE

I have written these fifteen Guides (Haikus and Prayers on the Ahl Al Kisa members as well as the Twelve Imams) via the inspiration that came to me while listening to one of the talks from Shaykh Muhammad Al-Yaqoubi Al-Hassani (qs) about the Dalial Ul-Khayrat, The Guide to Goodness written by Muhammad Sulyman b. Jazuli (qs). It inspired me so much knowing that sending peace and blessings upon Muhammad (ﷺ) is immensely beneficial and beautiful for the one sending blessings and peace upon him (ﷺ), so why not do the same for his (ﷺ) Ahl Al Bayt?

Hence the name of this small and sincere attempt at a book of prayers upon the purified ones. May it be accepted. Ameen 3x. All actions are according to the intentions as per the hadith of our Prophet (ﷺ). May this intention be accepted. Ameen x3. Do Khayr (Goodness), this is how you reach the soul of all worship, if Allah ﷻ, The One Supreme, so wills it to Be.

Any mistakes in this book are from me and any goodness in this book is from Allah ﷻ, The One Supreme, The Best, so forgive me and praise/worship Him, The Best, Allah ﷻ, The One Supreme, alone.

Imam ash-Shafi'i's Poem On The Ahl Al Bayt:

"يا أهل بيت رسول الله حبّكم فرض من الله في القرآن أنزله كفاكم من عظيم القد أنكم من لم

يصل عليكم لا صلوة له."

"O members of the Household (Ahl-al-Bayt) of the Messenger of Allah! (Our) love for you is an obligation, which God has revealed in the Qur'an. Your lofty station such that if one does not invoke blessings on you (while offering prayers) one's prayer will be of no avail."

(As-Sawa'iq al-Mahriqah, Book 11, Chapter 1, p. 148; Shabrawi, Al-Ithaf, p. 29; Hamzawi Maliki, Mashariq al-Anwar, p. 88; Zarqani, Al-Mawahib; Sabban, Al-As'af, p. 119)

THE GUIDES TO THE PROPHETIC HOUSEHOLD

SAQIBI SEIF

Ahl Al Kisa

According to the hadith of the Kisa, at least on one occasion, the Islamic prophet, Muhammad gathered his daughter Fatima, her husband Ali, and their two sons Hasan and Husayn, under his cloak, and then prayed, "O God, these are my Ahl Al Bayt (lit. 'the people of my house') and my closest family members; remove defilement from them and purify them completely," where this last statement is a reference to verse 33:33 of the Qur'an, known also as the verse of purification. These five have thus become known as the Ahl Al Kisa (lit. 'people of the cloak'). Variants of this tradition can be found in Sahih Muslim, Sunan al-Tirmidhi, and Musnad Ahmad ibn Hanbal, all canonical collections in Sunni Islam.

The Ahl Al Bayt

Parts of whole-why not?
here I, a presence of flow
swimming amongst it.

Oh Allah ﷲ, The One Supreme, send peace and blessings upon the Ahl Al Bayt, the light of lights, the parts of Whole/Oneness (Tawheed {Oneness}), may we be continuously embraced by their lights, the essence of our good fate, Ameen x3, the shining brilliance of Muhammad Ali Muhammad, as much as You send peace and blessings in all of Your heavens, as much as there is light from Your honorable presence, here the "I" swimming amongst it: the ocean of endless divine mysteries, heavenly favors, the light of lights, for You are the Majestic One, The One Supreme!

Ameen x3

The Twelve Holy Imams of Guidance

Ali Ibn Abi Talib (عَلَيْهِ الْسَّلام)

Hasan Ibn Ali (عَلَيْهِ الْسَّلام)

Husayn Ibn Ali (عَلَيْهِ الْسَّلام)

Ali Ibn Husayn Al-Sajjad (عَلَيْهِ الْسَّلام)

Muhammad Al-Baqir (عَلَيْهِ الْسَّلام)

Ja'far Al-Sadiq (عَلَيْهِ الْسَّلام)

Musa Al-Kadhim (عَلَيْهِ الْسَّلام)

Ali Al-Rida (عَلَيْهِ الْسَّلام)

Muhammad Al-Taqi (عَلَيْهِ الْسَّلام)

Ali Al-Hadi (عَلَيْهِ الْسَّلام)

Hasan Al-Askari (عَلَيْهِ الْسَّلام)

Muhammad Al-Mahdi (عَلَيْهِ الْسَّلام)

Sayyedina Muhammad Mustafa (ﷺ)

Some itch for its peace
some joyfully dance for it
a full-moon. The grace.

Oh Allah ﷻ, The One Supreme, send peace and blessings upon Muhammad ﷺ, Your حبيب ﷺ Crown wherein rests Jewels of infinite lights from the Will of Allah ﷻ, The One Supreme, reflected in the shining brilliance of Muhammad Ali Muhammad, the peace of the universes known and unknown, the galaxies dance/twirl from its joy, witnessing the full-moon of grace, as much as light shines, as much as darkness darkens, as much as You grant victory to the victors, the defeat to the ones defeated, for You are the Majestic One, The One Supreme!

Ameen x3

Imam Ali Ibn Abi Talib (عَلَيهِ الْسَّلام)

The first sign of sun!
dead snakes shall be seen
roses the weather.

Oh Allah الله, The One Supreme, send peace and blessings upon Imam Ali (عَلَيهِ الْسَّلام), the Crown Jewel of Truth from the heart of Mahmoud ﷺ, the shining brilliance of Muhammad Ali Muhammad, as much as creatures begin in Your Name, as much as there is to quantify and not to quantify, as much as You shine light, The Sun of Divine Truth حق, upon the falsehood aka the snakes, revealing their slithering depths, burning aflame their hisses of ignorance, purified from their deception, leaving nothing but rosy truths, as much as You are and forever will be, for You are the Majestic One, The One Supreme!

Ameen x3

Sayyeda Fatima Al-Zahra (عَلَيها الْسَّلام)

A grave that lives on!
A ghost enters into it
the sound of life now.

Oh Allah الله, The One Supreme, send peace and blessings upon Sayyeda Fatima Al-Zahra, the splendid one (عَلَيها الْسَّلام), the one who/Hu هو is a part of Mustafa ﷺ and Mustafa ﷺ a part of Fatima Al-Zahra, the hidden grave; the hidden Ka'ba, the direction of all saintly ones, hidden ones, known ones, the shining brilliance of Muhammad Ali Muhammad, as much as You create parts, as much as You create wholeness, as much as there is unity, life, as much as there is disunity, death, for You are the Majestic One, The One Supreme!

Ameen x3

Sayyeda Zainab Bint Ali (عَلَيها الْسَّلام)

Hello there my I
nothing seems to be ours
why does I not my?

Oh Allah ﷲ, The One Supreme, send peace and blessings upon Sayyeda Zainab (عَلَيها الْسَّلام), the one who/Hu هو is the champion of all things True, the daughter of the king of all Muslims, Imam Ali (عَلَيها ألْسَلام), basking in Truth's Wilayah (Sainthood), the shining brilliance of Muhammad Ali Muhammad, as much as You create champions, the multitudes of "I", the "I" is The Champion, albeit I don't own it, The Champion owns "I", as much as You create losers, as much as there is loss, as much as there is gain, for You are the Majestic One, The One Supreme!

Ameen x3

Imam Hasan Ibn Ali (عَلَيهِ الْسَّلام)

Roaming cities now
a wonder for wanderers
strolling the desert.

Oh Allah ﷲ, The One Supreme, send peace and blessings upon Imam Hasan (عَلَيهِ الْسَّلام), a flower in Your حبيب's heart's garden ﷺ, the garden of gardens wherein blossoms the most fragrant, beatific, and heavenly smells, the delight of delights, sweetening the cities with organic spirits of light, giving life to the lifeless, giving wonder to the wanderers, the oasis in the desert making the stroll ever so endearing, the shining brilliance of Muhammad Ali Muhammad, as much as You create delights, as much as goodness remains, as much as badness perishes, as much as clarity clarifies, for You are the Majestic One, The One Supreme!

Ameen x3

Imam Husayn Ibn Ali (عَلَيهِ الْسَّلام)

How bitter and sweet
thoughts and feelings; stormy and calm
taking everything.

Oh Allah الله, The One Supreme, send peace and blessings upon Imam Husayn (عَلَيهِ الْسَّلام), the Crown Jewel of Faith from the heart of Mustafa ﷺ the shining brilliance of Muhammad Ali Muhammad, as much as You created the lovers of Truth, as much as You create, as much as You create thoughts and feelings, as much as You take and give, as much as there is sweetness in the name Muhammad and Ali Muhammad, as much as there is injustice, Yazeed, and justice, Imam Husayn (عَلَيهِ الْسَّلام), and as much as Your Greatness demands, for You are the Majestic One, The One Supreme!

Ameen x3

Imam Muhammad Al-Baqir (ﻋَﻠَﻴﻪِ الْسَّلامﻋ)

Beginning with it
the men of last forever
ending with the start.

Oh Allah ﷲ, The One Supreme, send peace and blessings upon Imam Muhammad Al-Baqir (ﻋَﻠَﻴﻪِ الْسَّلامﻋ), the intelligent one, the shining brilliance of Muhammad Ali Muhammad, as much as You create intelligence, as much as You create dumbness, as much as You create awe, as much as You create beginnings, as much as You create such destination of men, as much as there is jadedness, as much as You create the endings of the beginnings of men, for You are the Majestic One, The One Supreme!

Ameen x3

Imam Ja'far Al-Sadiq (عَلَيهِ الْسَّلام)ُ

Guidance to guide now
guide to guidance forever
leaves blow in the wind.

Oh Allah الله, The One Supreme, send peace and blessings upon Imam Ja'far Al-Sadiq (عَلَيهِ الْسَّلام)ُ, the teacher of the teachers, the shining brilliance of Muhammad Ali Muhammad, as much as You create teachers, as much as You create students, as much as You create the idle ones, as much as there is beneficial knowledge, as much as You create guidance, as much as You create leafs that fall and flow in Your knowledge, as much as the winds gust forth, for You are the Majestic One, The One Supreme!

Ameen x3

Imam Musa Al-Kadhim (عَلَيهِ الْسَّلام)

Skinny day always
the moment in need of cake
movement never it.

Oh Allah الله, The One Supreme, send peace and blessings upon Imam Musa Al-Kadhim (عَلَيهِ الْسَّلام), the imprisoned and patient one, the shining brilliance of Muhammad Ali Muhammad, as much as You create patience, as much as You create imprisonment, as much as You create the freedom, as much as there is contemplation, as much as You fatten the past with thought, as much as You starve the moment of any worldly sweetness for those without gratitude, as much as the moment never moves out of its place, for You are the Majestic One, The One Supreme!

Ameen x3

Imam Ali Al-Rida (عَلَيهِ الْسَّلام)

Words flow like butter
Writing the Unwritten One
Winter no more now.

Oh Allah ﷲ, The One Supreme, send peace and blessings upon Imam Ali Al-Rida (عَلَيهِ الْسَّلام), the compiler of the Qur'an, the shining brilliance of Muhammad Ali Muhammad, as much as You create compilers, as much as the Qur'an intercedes for the ummah (nation), as much as You distribute the Qur'an, as much as the intercession of the Prophet Ahmed ﷺ reaches, as much as there is need, for You are the Majestic One, The One Supreme!

Ameen x3

Imam Muhammad Al-Taqi (عَلَيهِ الْسَّلام)

Note the noble ones
noble ones the Divine note
heavenly breezes.

Oh Allah الله, The One Supreme, send peace and blessings upon Imam Muhammad Al-Taqi (عَلَيهِ الْسَّلام), the charitable one, the shining brilliance of Muhammad Ali Muhammad, as much as You create wealth, as much as You create the needy ones, as much as You distribute the ways of the Ahl Al Bayt and to the Ahl Al Bayt, as much as their lights encompass existence/creation, as much as existence/creation points to the Prophet Ahmed ﷺ, for You are the Majestic One, The One Supreme!

Ameen x3

Imam Ali Al-Hadi (عَلَيهِ السَّلام)

Drunk upon sin now
the members of light sober
Rain quenches flowers.

Oh Allah الله, The One Supreme, send peace and blessings upon Imam Ali Al-Hadi (عَلَيهِ السَّلام), the sober one, the shining brilliance of Muhammad Ali Muhammad, as much as You create sobriety, as much as You create intoxicants, as much as You know, as much as You forgive, for You are the Majestic One, The One Supreme!

Ameen x3

Imam Hasan Al-Askari (عَلَيهِ الْسَّلام)

A prayer to God now
A member of God prays
Storm of truth accepts.

Oh Allah الله, The One Supreme, send peace and blessings upon Imam Hasan Al-Askari (عَلَيهِ الْسَّلام), the one whose bones are in all pure ones, the one whose prayers are accepted without any need of anything but love/relation to Mustafa ﷺ, the shining brilliance of Muhammad Ali Muhammad, as much as You create purity, as much as You create impurity, as much as You accept, as much as You reject, for You are the Majestic One, The One Supreme!

Ameen x3

Imam Muhammad Al-Mahdi (أُعَلَيهِ الْسَّلام)

An adult stare now
with a seraphic moment
becoming a boy.

Oh Allah الله, The One Supreme, send peace and blessings upon Imam Mahdi (أُعَلَيهِ الْسَّلام), the guiding one, the source of shining brilliancy of Muhammad Ali Muhammad, as much as You create brilliance, as much as You create the light, as much as You disperse guidance, the unveilings of the Ahl Al Bayt, as much as their lights and unveilings envelop life of the Prophet Mustafa ﷺ and all of his ﷺ touches, for You are the Majestic One, The One Supreme!

Ameen x3

اِللَّهُمَّ صل عَلَى مُحَمَّدٍ وَعَلَى آلِ مُحَمَّد

Allahumma Salli Ala Muhammad Wa Ala
Ali Muhammad

O Allah! Bless Muhammad and the family of
Muhammad.

FINAL THOUGHTS

I hope that these fifteen Guides (Haikus and Prayers on the Ahl Al Kisa members as well as the Twelve Imams) that are written for lovers of Truth opens and purifies/heals our bodies, minds, spirits, hearts, and souls so that we may reach the Divinely Presence unadulterated by the filth of falsehood.

We cannot fathom the support and lights of such guides in their totality, even just its glimmers of light are enough to drown all the universes in divine drunkenness, so therefore there's nothing left to say but this: Ya Ali Madad! Ya Ali Madad! Ya Ali Madad! May each reading of this book of guides to the prophetic household guide us and grant us the love of such loved ones, the love that will get us closer to The Best and be a means of incomprehensible blessings, safety, and mercy for us all here, in our graves, and hereafter.

Ameen x3

GLOSSARY OF ARABIC TEXT

ﷺ = Sallallahu Alayhi Wasallam (peace be upon him and his family {s})

'عَلَيهِ الْسَّلام = Alayhi As-Salaam "(as)" (peace be upon him)

عَلَيها الْسَّلام = Alayha As-Salaam "(as)" (peace be upon her)

هو = Hu (Is-ness, but its secret is limitless)

حبيب = Beloved